Copyright © 2016 Chantal R Wynter

All rights reserved. No part of this book may be used or reproduced by any means, graphic, electronic, or mechanical, including photocopying, recording, taping or by any information storage retrieval system without the written permission of the author except in the case of brief quotations embodied in critical articles and reviews.

Previously published as *Women in Government: 10 Key Strategies to Advance Your Career*

ISBN: 978-0-9971690-2-7

DEDICATION

This book is dedicated to my husband, parents, family, friends, and mentors, who never stopped believing in me. Thank you for your continued support.

This book is also dedicated to those who have a dream. Being an author was a dream of mine, and now it is a reality. If your dream is to advance your career, it is possible and my hope is that this book will help you on that journey.

CONTENTS

Acknowledgements. 6

Introduction: A Word From The Author. 8

How To Get Your First Leadership Position 13

Strategy 1: Have The Right Mindset
And Attitude 26

Strategy 2: Find Your Niche/Passion 42

Strategy 3: Get A Mentor. 49

Strategy 4: Network! Network! Network! 58

Strategy 5: Find A Sponsor 71

Strategy 6: Control Your Emotions
And Manage Your Stress 78

Strategy 7: Show Initiative, Volunteer,
And Go Above & Beyond. 99

Strategy 8: Be Prepared And Remain Prepared . 102

Strategy 9: Reputation And Perception 117

Strategy 10: Apply & Do It 122

Tips For Leaders 127

Bibliography 133

About The Author 136

ACKNOWLEDGEMENTS

I would like to acknowledge all the leaders that were instrumental in the creation of this book. Your knowledge and advice is priceless.

- Alia M. Shabazz
- Carole Cimitile
- Carolyn McMillon
- Courtni Berry
- Emily Liddel
- Erin McKee
- Glynnis Shane
- Interviewee A
- JoAnne McNabb
- Kaytura Felix
- Madonna Radcliff
- Natalya Komarova
- Rhonda Smith
- Ruth Zimmerman
- Shontal Linder

INTRODUCTION: A WORD FROM THE AUTHOR

"Life is like a combination lock;
your job is to find the right numbers, in the right order, so you can have anything you want."
– Brian Tracy

Have you ever wondered how some people are able to advance their career and others stagnate? In this book, I will discuss some of the strategies I have used as well as those used by the leaders I interviewed to propel our careers forward.

My journey to write this book began when I landed my first leadership position within the federal government. I was able to advance quickly within my agency by implementing key strategies I learned in my education, training, and on-the-job experience.

I am a young African American female in her late-20s leading and supervising at least three generations ranging from millennials like myself to baby boomers.

This is possible because of my tenacity, ambitions, and strategies highlighted in this book. When I started this book, I was an assistant supervisor but by implementing the strategies discussed, I am now a supervisor (within seven months).

This book-writing journey started as my attempt to identify obstacles faced by women in government and document the strategies used to overcome those obstacles and promote career growth. As a new leader, I worked to learn from other successful leaders in order to be the best leader possible. To do so, I interviewed 15 leaders ranging from new leaders to director level leaders. These leaders came from numerous agencies ranging from Drug Enforcement Administration (DEA) to Centers for Disease Control and Prevention (CDC). Surprisingly, I found that there were no obstacles specific to women leaders in government. The obstacles faced by women in government were the same across many working sectors (private, government, non-profit, etc.). Interestingly, some of the leaders felt that the government is a better place for women to work due to the standards, rules and regulations (such as equal employment opportunities and annual training requirements), and a greater availability of opportunities at a younger age due to hiring processes and procedures.[1]

During my interviews, I indentified 10 key strategies crucial for career advancement. This book discusses these strategies in full details while providing action items to help you get started.

I was always taught that knowledge is power and there are no guarantees in life. All we can do is prepare the best we can. The information and know-how of these strategies are powerful tools if applied. The strategies outlined in this book are strategies that worked for the leaders I interviewed and myself. Put yourself out there and use these strategies to assist you in getting into leadership and advancing once you get there.

No matter what, there are two things to remember, (1) take responsibility for your own career and (2) build relationships. Many of the strategies discussed in this book relate to relationships with yourself and with others. Therefore, take the time to build and maintain an honest relationship with yourself and those around

---

1   Interviews by telephone and email from June 2015 to July 2015

you. Do not wait or expect that others will pull you up and build your career.

Your career is your life, therefore, be prepared to fight for it.

HOW TO GET YOUR FIRST LEADERSHIP POSITION

Purpose: The purpose of this chapter is to identify strategies to help you get your first leadership position.

Nothing in life is guaranteed.

The best we can do is try our best, be as prepared as possible, and let the rest play itself out (this can be either through faith or luck – if you believe in one or the other).

The strategies outlined in this book are things that have worked for the leaders I interviewed as well as for myself. There are many underlying soft skills that are needed or would be beneficial in order to advance, such as your personality, communication skills, smiling, etc. Some of these will be addressed in this book.

Conducting these interviews, it became clear to me that ***one of the crucial aspects for getting your first***

CHAPTER 1:
HOW TO GET YOUR FIRST LEADERSHIP POSITION

leadership position is to master the technical skills of your non-leadership position. Many of the leaders I spoke to described how they were able to transition into leadership because of their skillset(s) and due to the fact that they were good at their jobs. Interviewee, *Erin McKee* stated she was able to land her first leadership position because she paid attention, was engaged, and performed. This all lead to her work speaking for itself.[2]

The 10 strategies in this book will assist you in landing your first leadership role if applied. These strategies work best when applied together.

When attempting to obtain your first leadership role fear of the unknown is a hurdle for many of us. One of the biggest lessons that one of the interviewees shared with me is that:[3]

> *The best motivator to do excellent work is FEAR.*

---

2   McKee, Erin, Telephone Interview, June 30, 2015

3   Interviewee A (anonymous), Telephone Interview, July 1, 2015

Fear is a gift of life; what you do with it stems from within and the mindset you have.

Tactic 1: *Overcome your psychological hurdle and roadblocks internally created.*

No one is perfect but we impose this expectation on ourselves, which can hinder our potential or push us to greatness. As leaders, at times we are required to make decisions and take risks based on limited information. Sometimes mistakes are made but **mistakes are just experiences**.[4] The key is that we do not keep making the same mistakes. Somehow, we must find a way to balance the risk, the limited information, and the need for perfection while remaining confident.

Interviewee, *Carolyn McMillon* explained how failure is a part of success.[5] She described a time when she participated in an outdoor training class, which forced her to take on various challenges outside her comfort zone with the risk of failure always looming

---

4   McMillon, Carolyn, Telephone and email interview, June 8 & 19, 2015

5   Ibid

around. Through this experience, she was taught a quote she always remembers:[6]

> *"There is no growth in the comfort zone and no comfort in the growth zone."*

She reminds herself of this saying each time she is faced with a challenge and it has been very effective for her.

In order for us to experience growth, we must be willing to step out of our comfort zone. For me, when I moved from one city to another within my agency it was a big risk but it paid off because I am excelling in my new city and job. The move led to the opportunity to become a formal leader within my agency, which may have taken a longer time, or not occurred at all if I stayed in my old city. Each uncomfortable step I took was a strategic career move. For example, stepping out of my comfort zone and going to events where I do not know anyone is a networking decision because it would

---

6   McMillon, Carolyn, Telephone and email interview, June 8 & 19, 2015

be easier and much preferred to stay home. However, in the end, I am always rewarded for stepping out my comfort zone because I am able to meet new people and learn something. You never know where you will make a connection and where it can take you. For example, because I stepped out of my comfort zone, joined a professional organization, attended meetings, and volunteered at an event, I was able to meet my mentor who has made my dream of being an author come true. You never know where and how you will meet your destiny. Do not be afraid to try things and take risks.

One interviewee shared how she was offered her dream job that she really wanted; but she was terrified that she would fail and feared she would be hired to be fired.[7] Yes – she feared she would be hired to be fired! Already, she had failure as her mindset, which would have been her destiny. However, she spoke with one of her mentors who pointed out that the feeling of fear is real but the voice is wrong. Her mentor explained that anyone who has excelled at a job has been afraid; without fear there is no motivation to truly succeed. Fear can either cripple us or motivate us. Once we

---

[7]   Interviewee A (anonymous), Telephone Interview, July 1, 2015

CHAPTER 1:
HOW TO GET YOUR FIRST LEADERSHIP POSITION

realize that we can do what we set our minds to, when we achieve it, we must own it.

> *Don't be afraid to own and voice your idea.*

To help you along, it is crucial to have people who believe in you because sometimes you will need others telling you that you can do it before you start believing in yourselves. Get out of your mind and stop limiting your potential because of fear. Change your mindset to realize fear is a motivator and it will help you to accomplish your goals. Fear is not bad, it is good.

> *Fear is not about actually doing the work; fear is the anticipation of what may go wrong.*

The fear and anticipation of what you consider to be undesirable is probably worse than the reality. Once you're able to overcome the psychological hurdle of fear, you're able to see that you can do it. Once you're able to move pass the fear and successfully accomplish or overcome what you once feared, it becomes easier and easier. Then the next time you're faced with a fearful task, you can reference the time when fear motivated you and you were successful. For example, I recall a time at work when I had to inform my new employees that annual leave was up to the discretion of the agency and could be denied. I was extremely fearful because I knew the employees would not like what I had to say and would have questions. Therefore, I took the time to determine how I could deliver the message in the best tone possible. I found written guidance and read this to the employees while explaining the reasoning behind the policy. The employees, while they did not like or agree with what I had to say, respected that I had the reference and understood the rationale. In the end, I said to myself, "see that wasn't so bad." From that point forward, I was able to rationalize fear with a new mindset because fear pushed me to find documentation and the best way to deliver the message to my new employees.

> **ACTION ITEM**
>
> **Let fear be the driving force to make you better.**

Let fear be the driving force to make you better. If you are thinking about applying for that job, do it. Don't be afraid to fail. Even if you fail, you can learn

CHAPTER 1:
HOW TO GET YOUR FIRST LEADERSHIP POSITION

from the experience and do better the next time. If you never try, you won't have the experience to learn from. Imagine if you didn't fail; what would that mean to you? Think about it! Hopefully, the thought of succeeding creates hope in your heart and mind and motivates you to do it. Put yourself out there. There is no growth in the comfort zone and no comfort in the growth zone.[8]

In the end, you have to be comfortable in your own skin and trust that you know what you need to know[9] and that it will be enough. Be confident and have the expectation that you will be great. Sometimes, we just have to have faith and the 10 strategies in this book will give you extra assistance.

Tactic 2: *Show your supervisor that you are an excellent employee willing to work hard for the agency.*

Do this with a smile and on a consistent basis. Remain focus on your goal(s) and the agency's mission. Consistency is the key.

---

8   McMillon, Carolyn, Telephone and email interview, June 8 & 19, 2015

9   Shabazz, Alia M, Telephone Interview, July 2, 2015

Tactic 3: *Let your supervisor and those in management know that you are interested in leading.*

Later on, I will discuss the power of having a sponsor and what it can mean for your advancement. However, first it starts with putting a voice to your ambitions and goals. It is all about planting as many seeds as you can and nurturing those seeds until they grow to fruition. You plant seeds by telling the right people about your ambitions. It is great to know your ambitions, but others cannot help you to get to where you want to be without knowing where you want to go. The help of others is needed for career advancement.

> *If you do not ask people for help, you may be robbing them of the chance they desire to be helpful.*

Asking for help may be a painful task for some, but there are indirect ways to do this. For example, you don't have to directly ask your supervisor for assistance, you can simply make it known that you are interested in leadership and/or management in passing and continue to show expertise at your job. Remember, a good supervisor develops their employees. I understand that some of you may be uncomfortable informing others of your goals; however, this is a crucial tactic to get into leadership and to advance up the leadership ranks. Do not assume that people will notice your hard work and promote you. ***Your hard work without a voice to your goals may hinder you because management will recognize your value in your current position and may not think to move you out of your position.***

Lastly, create a career plan with your supervisor and seek their buy-in. In my agency, this is called an Individual Development Plan (IDP). Whatever it is called in your agency, participate in this exercise and create a plan clearly outlining your goals and steps that can be taken to get you where you want to be.

Tactic 4: *Build your non-technical skills.*

Apply, volunteer, and take leadership classes or programs. These classes and programs will not only build your technical skills but will serve as a networking opportunity and demonstrate to upper management how serious you are about your

> **ACTION ITEM**
>
> **Demonstrate the competencies for the job you are seeking while in your current job.**

aspirations. In addition, it is advised that you begin to demonstrate the necessary competencies for the job you are seeking to transition into. This will show management that you are able to do the job and to begin seeing you in that job.

Here are some key advice shared from the interviewees that can help you to get your first leadership position and advance:

o Interviewee, *Glynnis Shane* states your reputation is crucial. Try not to fall into any cliques or be surrounded by negativity. Be known as the person who goes above and beyond and is available to lend a hand.[10]

o Interviewee, *Alia M. Shabazz* encourages carrying yourself in a manner that your supervisor does not have to worry about you or question what you are doing.[11]

o Leaders don't want the details or want you to speak bad about others. Leaders want you to speak to the business. Show your leaders that you are a valued

---

10   Shane, Glynnis, Telephone Interview, June 26, 2015

11   Shabazz, Alia M, Telephone Interview, July 2, 2015

member of the organization by being honest and always remember to frame it in the context of your agency's mission.[12]

- Interviewee *Kaytura Felix* states you should answer this question: Why should you be promoted? [13]

  - If you don't have an answer – work on getting an answer.

  - If you have an answer, does it relate back to the agency? Does anyone know you're interested in being promoted?

- Dress for the job you want not for the job you have. This will show all those in management that you are serious about advancing and it will help them to picture you within the management ranks. Dressing for the job you want is a visual cue and a reminder to management that you are serious about your ambitions. In addition, your dress code will lend itself to your reputation and to your career goals.

The 10 strategies discussed to help you get your first

---

12 Shabazz, Alia M, Telephone Interview, July 2, 2015

13 Felix, Kaytura, Telephone Interview, July 6, 2015

leadership position and advance your career are as follows:

1. Have the right mindset and attitude.
2. Find your niche/passion.
3. Get a mentor.
4. Network, network, network!
5. Find a sponsor.
6. Control your emotions and manage your stress.
7. Show initiative, volunteer, and go above and beyond.
8. Be prepared and remain prepared.
9. Be aware of your reputation and others' perception of you.
10. Apply and do it!

STRATEGY 1: HAVE THE RIGHT MINDSET AND ATTITUDE

Purpose: Emphasize and elaborate on the power of the right mindset and attitude.

"75% of job successes are predicted by your optimism levels, your social support, and your ability to see stress as a challenge instead of a threat."
– Shawn Anchor, Author of *the Happiness Advantage*

The mind is a powerful tool.

I have been faced with adversity and challenges throughout my life. Migrating to the US without my mother and leaving behind everything I was accustomed to at the age of 10 was a challenge and an obstacle but I learned to adapt. As a young, African American female attempting to enter and advance into leadership, I faced obstacles. I had to overcome my insecurities, stereotypes, others' perception of me, my doubts, my fears, and roadblocks put in place by others (which were out of my control). I did not let these obstacles and challenges deter me from my dream. As I write this book, my thoughts occasionally drift to the negativity of the what ifs that may or may not occur. When I find my mind doing this, I make an effort to switch my thoughts to focus on all the positive what ifs. For example, instead of focusing on what if no one buys this book, I focus on what if this book becomes a best seller. Then I imagine how I would feel. I think about how happy I would be and how proud it would make me. Instead of focusing on what if my employees dislike me and I am unable to motivate them, I focus on what if my employees respect and admire me and are motivated to work for me. For all the potential negatives, there is a positive. Even if there is a negative outcome, positivity can shine through. Napoleon Hill once said, "every adversity, every failure, every heartache carries with it the seed of an equal or greater benefit." Meeting a negative outcome with the right mindset can teach us a lesson, make us stronger and/ or wiser, and help to make the positive outcomes more

> **ACTION ITEM**
>
> **Train your mind to counteract each negative thought with a positive thought.**

CHAPTER 2:
STRATEGY 1: HAVE THE RIGHT MINDSET AND ATTITUDE

enjoyable and appreciated. The mind is a powerful tool and by transmitting positive energy, positivity will surround you.

Take for example, a crucial organ – your eyes. It is recommended that we check our vision every one to two years depending on your risk factors and age (according to the American Optometric Association),[14] however, how often do you do a mental/mindset check-up? At the vision check-ups, if you wear any corrective devices, fine-tuning may be needed in order to improve your vision. The same policy applies to your mindset. Certain fine-tuning may be required to improve your quality of life and advance your career. It is highly recommended that you routinely evaluate your mindset, either twice a year, yearly, or every two years to determine where you stand and what can be improved. Sometimes, a new perspective or lens is needed in order to grow and advance.

---

14   http://www.aoa.org/patients-and-public/caring-for-your-vision/comprehensive-eye-and-vision-examination/recommended-examination-frequency-for-pediatric-patients-and-adults?sso=y

> *Looking at your life and career through a new lens or focus can open up opportunities and options that were invisible before.*[15]

For example, how would you handle a situation where a co-worker was making your work life experience miserable and you had to move to another unit or location? Would you fuss because you had to start over in a new area or be excited for a fresh start to meet new people and build new skills? As I mentioned before, the mind is a powerful tool. Do not waste it thinking negatively or having a limited outlook. Take on multiple perspectives and see the upside in all that happens to you. In each event, there is a lesson. ***In order to advance your career, you have to first believe that you are capable and ready to take on the additional duties required.*** It is important to be driven and know that it is possible to advance in your career. With this belief, the right mindset, attitude, and tools, your determination will be hard to break.

---

15 Felix, Kaytura, Telephone Interview, July 6, 2015

Confidence

Don't be afraid to speak up and stand up for your ideas and what you believe in. Get in the habit of participating. What do you have to lose if you participate?

> *Confidence is not arrogance; it is self-awareness and belief in one's self and capabilities.*

Don't let anyone or any situation take away your confidence. The daunting goal of perfection can chip away at your confidence level but it is important to not let it. The confidence and self-belief you have is a crucial ingredient in overcoming some of the biggest hurdles. In life, we may not have the support or supporters we need. Sometimes, the vision will start and end with you; however, with confidence and self-belief you can turn a vision into reality. I am a confident person. When others doubted me or looked at my age as being too young for management, I knew in my heart I was ready and I was confident in my abilities and what I could offer. Therefore, I did not need the belief of others; I had all the belief I needed. I used my confidence and belief to prepare, apply, and obtain my first leadership role.

You will encounter moments where your confidence level is low; however, you should never forget what you are capable of. Remind yourself of your greatest accomplishment or a time you overcame a challenge or obstacle. In your memory of this event, recall how successful you were and remind yourself that since you overcame that challenge/obstacle, you can do it again. Once you are able to knock down your first challenge/obstacle, you know you can do it every time.

Be confident enough to speak up and know your opinion matters; make your voice heard. If you speak up and you're not heard, remain engaged and speak up again. Trust yourself because you can do it. Don't be easily discouraged. Your voice matters and what you say matters. Never give up and be persistent. You matter; you can do it! Have hope and faith. With faith, anything is possible.

> **ACTION ITEM**
>
> **Participate and speak up.**

*Confidence **is a mindset and an attitude***. If you happen to lack the necessary confidence needed

CHAPTER 2:
STRATEGY 1: HAVE THE RIGHT MINDSET AND ATTITUDE

to advance your career, it is possible to obtain that confidence with the correct tuning. Confidence is a skill that can be learned and mastered. For some, confidence will come easy while for others it will take a little work. Some techniques to help build self-confidence include believing in yourself or having faith in yourself, exuding the illusion of self-confidence until you are no longer giving the illusion, and reminding yourself of all the things you can do. In addition, practice walking with your head held high, a straight posture, as well as dressing in a confident manner. As they say, sometimes we have to fake it until we make it.

Previously, I shared the action – ***Train your mind to counteract each negative thought with a positive thought.*** This action item also applies to building confidence. Do not doubt yourself and surround yourself with negative thoughts and people who do not believe in you. Surround yourself with people who exude confidence and before you realize it, you will transform into someone with confidence. Even when you are in unfamiliar territory, always say to yourself, I can do this and I have the resources to be successful.[16] Not being 100% positive you can do something, does

---

16 Interviewee A (anonymous), Telephone Interview, July 1, 2015

not have to stop you from actually doing it. Take this risk on yourself; you deserve it. A lack of confidence can be a detriment to any career. Employers want people who are confident and competent to do the assigned job or task. They do not want someone who will constantly second guess themselves and be afraid.

In order to have confidence and the mindset for success in a leadership position, you must have a passion for what you do. Loving your work and enjoying the journey of enhancing your skills and honing your expertise will keep you in the correct mindset. Your attitude will remain positive if you take pleasure in what you do, which will be discussed further in the next chapter.

Understand your counterpart

Another tool crucial to having the right mindset and attitude is understanding the shortcomings of your counterparts and learning from your interactions with them. Understand that there will be people out there who will be unwilling to help you because they view you as a competition or undeserving of the job, regardless of your actual competencies. Retain this knowledge and remain professional. The acceptance of this information will prepare you mentally for any repercussions you will experience due to the advancement of your career. When I transitioned into management as the youngest person for my office among the current leadership, I was aware that people would question how I accomplished the promotion but I did not let it bother or deter me because I knew I worked hard to get where I was. I'd prepared my mind and thoughts to handle this blowback; therefore, it had no effect on me when I heard it. I remained professional and kept my emotions in check, not allowing other people's thoughts or beliefs to change my mindset.

Refocus your mindset

The refocusing of your mindset is also needed when you make a mistake or interact with people that are trying to get a reaction from you. Once you have the proper mindset and reinforcement tools, mistakes, setbacks, and negativity will roll off you. Reinforcement tools include network and support (family, friends, mentors), educational support (books, lectures, podcast), motivational words (motivational speakers, daily quotes), visual cues (movies, pictures), and spiritual belief. Once you have a mixture of these in your toolbox, your mind and attitude will be hard to break.

Some of the other key valuable mindset advice shared from the leaders I interviewed include:

- Don't expect respect. Respect has to be earned.
- Know that the position you have or take will not always be liked and be okay with that.
- Practice servant leadership.
- Keep a journal.

Don't expect respect. Respect has to be earned

Basic respect can be expected for some based on their title. However, the deep rooted respect that comes with loyalty and unwavering support has to be earned. This level of respect can be earned by practicing servant leadership, which is discussed in this chapter. This type of respect doesn't happen overnight, it takes time and trust. Having the right attitude and mindset to know that you will have to work for the respect of those you lead will help to avoid a lot of headaches. The right mindset will also help to gain the deep rooted respect that goes well beyond the foundation respect.

CHAPTER 2:
STRATEGY 1: HAVE THE RIGHT MINDSET AND ATTITUDE

Know that the position you have or take, will not always be liked[17]

You will not be liked by everyone and you cannot please everyone. In the end, someone will get the short end of the stick, whether it is you or someone else depends on your mindset. As leaders, we must learn that we will not be liked by everyone and we have to be okay with this fact. I have struggled with this over the years and I had to adjust my attitude and mindset to know that first I must be happy within myself. Some people will not be your biggest fan but as long as you are content with yourself, then you can keep moving forward. Do not let the nay-sayers deter you from your path in life (career or not) and be positive when dealing with others.

Servant Leadership[18]

Servant leadership is leading by serving others. Through servant leadership, respect, trust, loyalty, admiration, and devotion can be earned. These emotions will be the glue among your team because

---

17   Zimmerman, Ruth, Telephone Interview, July 6, 2015

18   Felix, Kaytura, Telephone Interview, July 6, 2015

they will feel as if you have their backs and their best interest at heart. Servant leadership is understanding that your job as a leader is to serve your team's needs as well as the needs of your colleagues, supervisor, and agency. Through servant leadership, you can help to make the organization and/or your team better. As a result of servant leadership, you work in the best interest of your team and agency and not for yourself. Servant leadership puts the people you lead/serve first. Do so by ensuring you work alongside your employees and get involved. Do not be the leader who barks orders but will not step in and do the work. Servant leadership means leading by example. Show the level of work ethic you require by adhering to that level yourself. By shifting your mindset and redefining your primary job description to serving your organization, you can build stronger relationships. This mindset will help you to see the needs of your agency, to which you can then provide solutions. Interviewee, *Kaytura Felix* discusses this topic with great passion.[19] With this mindset, opportunities

> **ACTION ITEM**
>
> Ask yourself, "what can I do to fix this problem, help the agency, and help my employees?"

---

19   Felix, Kaytura, Telephone Interview, July 6, 2015

to volunteer your talents and address problems in your agency become apparent. You no longer look to complain about a problem, instead, you ask yourself, "what can I do to fix this problem and help the agency." This question that should be kept on your mind at all times.

Keep a Journal[20]

Journaling is an excellent tool to keep account of all that has transpired in your life. It is a powerful career tool as well as a tool to help you reflect on your mindset and the type of leader you are, were, or want to be. Journaling helps you to learn about yourself and see your blind spots. While it is good to allow others to help you identify your blind spots or areas for improvements, journaling can also assist in this area. Journaling helps to determine how we can be better leaders. In the beginning of this chapter, I alluded to the importance of a vision check-up. An optician has their tools to assist with the vision check-up, to help them identify areas of concerns and/or improvement. A journal can be used in the same manner as a self–check of our mindset and attitude.

---

20   Felix, Kaytura, Telephone Interview, July 6, 2015

Did you keep a journal when you were younger? I did and when I read back through my journals I am able to analyze my mindset and recall events that I experienced which I forgot about or didn't recall all the details. Reading my old journals helps me to see how much I have grown and what my dreams and ambitions were. The same applies to keeping a journal as an adult especially keeping a career journal. We spend most of our time working, why not document the journey? Use your journal as a tracking and assessment tool. You may be amazed at what you end up learning and remembering years from now with the help of your journal.

Some ideas for what you can write about in your journal include; a daily/weekly reflection, discussing what you have learned for the day or week, any disappointments or accomplishments, goals, challenges, books you have read, and key people you met for the day, week, or month.

> **ACTION ITEM**
>
> Keep a journal. Write down the questions you have and where you want to be in five years.

Have an optimistic mindset and perception on life and your career. This point of view will lead to

CHAPTER 2:
STRATEGY 1: HAVE THE RIGHT MINDSET AND ATTITUDE

opportunities and growth that you may have never imagined. Do not give up! The setbacks and the no's are only there to make you stronger and prepare you for your success.

> *Prepare for what you want, put a voice to your desires and dreams, and the rest will work itself out.*

This is my mindset and it has worked for me and many of the leaders I interviewed.

My mindset has been crucial to my success. I was able to advance quickly at a young age because I surrounded myself with people who believed in me and could motivate me to do better. I had the confidence necessary to convince others I was capable of doing the job and leading others. I can recall my first week as a leader in my job. I was scared and nervous. I wanted to be liked and to be successful. The employees I manage are unionized and in my first week, I had to sit down with the union because an employee didn't like a decision I made. Of course, this was nerve racking and I was scared but I remained optimistic. I learn the most through challenges. I am a woman of faith and I knew, I would only be given what I could handle and that there was a lesson to be learned. I didn't quit or let this mishap discourage me. Instead, I learned the lay of the land and the policies surrounding the conflict. It was a great learning moment that has helped me to be a better leader.

STRATEGY 2: FIND YOUR NICHE/PASSION

Purpose: Discuss the importance of doing what you love or what is unique to you.

> "The woman who follows the crowd will usually go no further than the crowd. The woman who walks alone is likely to find herself in places no one has ever been before."
> – Albert Einstein

Not only is it important to have the right mindset or attitude but it is also important to identify your passion(s); your niche.

Once you are able to identify your passion or purpose in life, life becomes more meaningful. It is a beautiful thing to enjoy what you do for "work". It doesn't feel like work, instead it feels as if you are doing something you were meant to do and you are at peace.

I asked all the interviewees, "What advice do you wish you knew starting/advancing your leadership career that would have better prepared you as a leader?"

Interviewee, Carolyn McMillon wrote:

> "I…wish I…understood more about my life's purpose earlier in my life. I advise you and others to create a purpose statement for your life. This will give you focus and direction, personally and professionally. I did not learn about creating my personal life purpose until later in life."

Another leader stated that, it's one thing to know it in your head but you need to know it in your heart.[21]

Recently, I stumbled upon my passion. Before this, I felt lost and without a clear focus. In college, I was afraid to pick a specific major because of the fear that I may miss out on something. I wanted to be talented at everything. However, I quickly learned that a jack of all trades did not work for me. I had drive and motivation but nowhere specific to point it. I had

---

21 Interviewee A (anonymous), Telephone Interview, July 1, 2015

CHAPTER 3:
STRATEGY 2: FIND YOUR NICHE/PASSION

to work hard and dig deep to identify what made me happy. The day I learned that people pay money for career coaching and talent development, I could not contain my joy. I can recall from high school how I was naturally gifted at helping to motivate others to greater limits, or assisting with resumes or interviews. I've had many people in my life thank me for guiding them and motivating them to be better. One friend gives me credit for motivating him to go to law school when he was at a low point in life. Looking back, I realize that without much thought I was always in the mix of helping others with their careers and talents. Now, I am writing this book to try to help as many people as possible to advance their career.

The beautiful thing about finding your niche, purpose, and/or passion is that it helps to boost your confidence and mindset. There is no other feeling than the one when you know you are doing what makes you happy and what you were put on this earth to do. Your passion will come to you easily or naturally. It is something that you find yourself doing frequently and you are good at. It will also be the thing that makes you happy. Sometimes, you may run into the roadblock of figuring out how to make a living doing what you love. That is okay! Just keep doing it, even if it is through volunteer work or at your church. To determine a way to make a profit with your talents, research and network. Researching will help you to get ideas and networking will help you to make connections and meet people who can assist. The importance of networking as well as how to network will be discussed in a later chapter.

On the other hand, your passion does not have to be something you use to make a profit. Your passion can be used to bring joy, purpose, and meaning in your life without ever making a profit. The decision between profit or not, is left to you.

If you have no clue what your passion or life's purpose is, here are two tips to help you find out.

- Constant self-reflection in order to learn who you are.
- Self-assessment tools.

Constant self-reflection in order to learn who you are

Getting to know who you are on an intimate level is very important. Figuring out the answers to the questions below is a great starting point to help you learn your passion.

1. What do you like and don't like?
   a. Example: nonprofit/government/corporate, entrepreneur, bureaucratic organizations, etc.
2. What are your strengths and weaknesses?
3. What are your negative and positive triggers?
4. What are your limits for what you will not stand for or accept in your career and in life?
5. What motivates you?
6. What is important to you?

To help answer some of these questions, you can learn by trial and error, practice, experience, mentors, volunteering, internships, shadow assignments and details, informational interviews, and career coach.

Self-assessment tools

Self-assessment tools are a great way to identify your passion and analyze who you are. These tools can help you to reflect and aide in your journey of revelation. Books are great self-assessment tools. There are many books that discuss the art of identifying your passion.

Some of the more popular self-assessment tools include,

- *Myers-Briggs Type Indicator*
- *DISC Personality Test*
- *MAPP Career Assessment Test*
- *180 and 360 Degree Assessment*
- *The Big Five Personality Test*
- *Riso-Hudson Enneagram Type Indicator*
- *Career Strengths Test*
- *Pymetrics*

ONET Online is also a great tool to use to explore careers based on certain work values. 123Test.com is another tool, which offers free assessments such as DISC Personality Test.

Conduct your own research by:

- Doing online search.
- Talking to experts and people doing what you are aspiring to do.
- Attend lectures.
- Join professional organizations focus on your interests.

It doesn't matter what you do as long as you are doing something that will help you to gain exposure and knowledge. In time, the answers you seek will appear. Whether you are spiritual or not, sometimes it will take faith and unwavering determination. My life's

CHAPTER 3:
STRATEGY 2: FIND YOUR NICHE/PASSION

motto is that everything happens for a reason. I am a firm believer that no matter what happens in my life, it's for a purpose. I believe there are lessons in everything. I remain optimistic and always find a new perspective to help me get one-step closer to my goal(s).

In your career, your passion and commitment will be the key ingredient to longevity and advancement. This is so you will naturally outshine others when you are doing what you love because you are naturally gifted in that field. Putting in the extra effort and time will be easy. Understand, that no one will hand you a leadership position, it will come down to who you know, what you have shown others, and going the extra mile. Interviewee, *Erin McKee* stated that it is important to identify what leadership looks like for you and then identify your strategy to achieve leadership.[22] It is also just as important not to change who you are. Rely on the strengths you were given, fine-tune them in order to advance, and maximize your strengths to be the best you can be.[23]

---

22 McKee, Erin, Telephone Interview, June 30, 2015

23 Liddel, Emily, Telephone Interview, July 7, 2015

STRATEGY 3: GET A MENTOR

Purpose: Discuss the benefits of a mentor, how to find a mentor, where to find a mentor, and how to build effective mentorships.

> "A mentor is someone who allows you to see the hope inside yourself."
> – Oprah Winfrey

One of my best mentors came at a time when I was struggling with the culture of the agency I worked for.

I sought out guidance and assistance (in other words, a mentor) from the director of the office. We got to know each other and he was willing to mentor me informally. On a monthly basis, we met up to catch up and discuss any topic whether work or personal. He offered books I could read, classes I could take, and started to groom me. As part of his grooming process, he introduced me to someone in leadership outside of the office. This relationship started more formally but

CHAPTER 4:
STRATEGY 3: GET A MENTOR

we worked on building a relationship and setting goals and expectations. This person then introduced me to a leadership program unfamiliar to my office and I was able to participate in the program. From there, I was introduced to another person in leadership to help guide me as I transitioned to a new office and started to think seriously about entering into leadership. From this mentorship, which started at a time when I was struggling, the seed for leadership was planted as well as the inspiration and belief that I would be a great leader.

My call for help led to meeting two leaders within my agency, a leadership program, growth in my network, and unmeasurable knowledge and guidance. You can never truly predict where a mentorship relationship can take you but the journey is always fun especially in an effective mentorship. The mentors I've had, all positively impacted my career and life in general.

There are different kinds of mentors and you can have more than one mentor. Personally, at any given time I've had three or four mentors I could pick up the phone and consult with. My mentors have different backgrounds and offer different perspectives. In addition, I've had formal and informal mentors.

Formally, meaning the relationship had structure and/or was initiated through a structured program like a leadership program and informally, as in a relationship with no set guidelines that is built on a personal connection.

Benefits of mentorship

A mentor can help you to learn the lay of the land. Some may call it the politics or the rules of the game but either way, if you can find someone to show you the dos and don'ts, this will save you a lot of time and help you to avoid crucial mistakes.

Finding a mentor at work is especially important because they can help you learn the work culture, pull you up the ranks,[24] and coach you for your next position within the agency by identifying what roles or experiences to gain. It is not what you know but who you know. If you are connected with the right people, what you know is just an added bonus to solidify the deal for your advancement. Therefore, having mentors helps you meet the right people and get insider knowledge. Your mentor can serve as someone to connect you with other influential people in your

---

24 Smith, Rhonda, Telephone Interview, June 16, 2015

agency. A mentor can also serve as a person to discuss ideas and to help motivate you. A mentor guides and assists you, as interviewee, *Carolyn McMillon* wrote:

> "Too frequently, as women, we have not made it a priority to seek out mentors and coaches for guidance and assistance in helping us to navigate our career paths. I strongly recommend the use of coaches and mentors early on and continuous throughout your career."[25]

How can you find a mentor?

Finding a mentor is easier than you think. Just ask! Many people want to feel as if they can make a difference. Therefore, most are willing to mentor you if they have the time and can make the commitment. Yes – mentoring is a commitment and should be treated as such. You want a mentor who will take the relationship seriously and has your best interest at heart.

---

25   McMillon, Carolyn, Telephone and email interview, June 8 & 19, 2015

While it is easy to just ask someone to be your mentor, it is important that you ask the right person. Be careful not to seek out a mentor that is dishonest or not trust worthy. Interviewee, *Ruth Zimmerman,* recommends finding someone that is willing to work with you and expose you to different ideas.[26]

Another interviewee shared some strategies she used to identify a mentor:[27]

- Find someone you admire. Then start an informal relationship or friendship. Invite the person to lunch and be honest to why you were drawn to that person. Then let the person know that you would love for he/she to be your mentor and assist you in getting from point A to B.

- This interviewee recommended that you only cultivate the mentorship relationship if the initial advice given was effective. Your time is a precious commodity; sticking around in a relationship that is not effective or beneficial is

---

26 Zimmerman, Ruth, Telephone Interview, July 6, 2015

27 Interviewee A (anonymous), Telephone Interview, July 1, 2015

a waste of time.

Where do you find a mentor?

- LinkedIn
- Work – on the job project, supervisor, or etc.
- Professional organizations
- Volunteer work
- Church
- Friends
- Family members
- Leadership programs
- School
- Conferences and lectures

As mentioned before, when selecting a mentor, I highly recommend having a mentor at work because they will be able to give you work/agency specific advice and they will have an understanding of the environment and what may or may not work. Not only is it important to seek a mentor at work but preferably one in leadership. As one of the interviewees pointed out, having a mentor in leadership allows you to have someone pull you up in the agency or groom you.

How to build an effective mentor relationship and what does it look like?

Your mentor should be a person who challenges you, introduces new ideas and concepts to you, pushes you out of your comfort zone, and as Oprah stated in the opening quote of this chapter, instills hope.

For example, I've had many mentors who introduced me to new leadership concepts, books, and to other leaders. In addition, my mentors have tailored their advice and guidance to my needs, whether they are books, projects, assignments, programs, or an introduction to certain people. This is an effective mentorship.

The duties of a mentor are not one that should be taken lightly and can be overwhelming.

> **ACTION ITEM**
>
> Have your mentor give you a list of people to meet within your agency and if possible, have them make an introduction.

Things to do to build an effective mentorship:

1. Build a relationship that is not just face value. Allow your mentor to get to know the real you. The more your mentor knows about you, the better that person will be able to assist you (whether that be identifying your strengths, finding opportunities for growth, knowing what you are ready for, how hard to push you, etc.).
2. Set goals and expectations.
3. Identify your needs and how your mentor can assist you.
4. Be open minded to the advice your mentor gives you.
5. Be present for the relationship.
6. Be willing to do the work.
7. Remain respectful.
8. Your mentor should be committed to you and your success.
9. Remain in contact with your mentor – send progress notes and life changes when necessary.
10. Be willing to lend a helping hand to your mentor.
11. Be accountable to your mentor and hold your mentor accountable.

Just as a mentor is important for your growth and development, you should do the same for others. Pass the torch and lend the helping hand. The impact your mentors have on your life, you can do the same for someone else and more.

STRATEGY 4: NETWORK! NETWORK! NETWORK!

Purpose: Identify the power of networking, the different ways to network, where to network, who to network with, when to network, and how to network successfully.

"I've learned that people will forget what you said, people will forget what you did, but people will never forget how you made them feel."
— Maya Angelou

Networking is not only about fulfilling your individual needs; it is also about fulfilling the needs of others and leaving a lasting impression.

As the quote by Maya Angelou discusses, people will remember you based on how you made them feel. In other words, the connection and/or relationship you are able to create and ignite in the minutes or hours spent together is what matters. I will share some of the techniques I have used throughout the years as well as techniques shared by the leaders I interviewed.

The art of networking has evolved. We no longer have to meet someone in person to be able to network. Now, networking also encompasses the virtual world. Networking is not a matter of instant gratification. It takes time to build a strong network and it takes work. When it is time to rely on your network, knowing the right people will prove to be very valuable. Networking has a compound effect, the more you invest, the more it grows. Therefore, spend time growing, developing, and feeding your network, because the return on your investment is priceless. Throughout my interviews, many of the leaders recommended starting the journey of networking early on. The fact that this is a common trend, speak volumes to the value of networking.

> *Start networking early, do it often, and invest the time and energy.*

CHAPTER 5:
STRATEGY 4: NETWORK! NETWORK! NETWORK!

The benefits of networking

Networking gives you a chance to build friendships with people from different backgrounds (experiences, business functions, etc.), obtain advice when needed, be informed, exposed and recommended for opportunities, and provides introduction to other people, especially to those that may be inaccessible.

One of the biggest benefits of networking is the career opportunities that can result. Interviewee, *Shontal Linder*, shared a key lesson she learned that was very important in her agency: "The more known I make myself, the better my chance will be in advancing my career."[28] In her agency and probably in many organizations, who you know is crucial. However, ***it is not just about who you know, it is who knows you***. Interviewee, *Kaytura Felix* stated, "if people don't know who you are, then how can they look out for you?"[29] This drives home the importance of networking. People cannot help you if they do not know you need help. Networking is an impactful method of getting others to know who you are. However, later on, I will discuss the strategy of perception and reputation because

---

28 Linder, Shontal, Telephone Interview, June 25, 2015

29 Felix, Kaytura, Telephone Interview, July 6, 2015

networking is a domino effect. Once person A knows you and you become an asset to them, it is inevitable, that person A will mention you to person B. Think of a good office gossip, you can use this phenomenon to your advantage by creating a stellar reputation. In addition, it is a skill to be able to identify who to open up to. Trust has to be earned but no matter what, be yourself.

You are who you associate with is a fact that applies directly with networking. Associate with leaders and their knowledge and attitude will eventually rub off on you. One interviewee shared that working with like-minded or inspirational people who support your goal is very powerful.[30] This is a tremendous confidence booster and motivational source.

Introduction to other people from your network, especially inaccessible people is priceless. Your network serves as a referral base. Think about all the times you have tried something based on the word of someone you knew or trusted. The same applies with our careers. People listen to people they know or trust. Therefore, if someone tells them that you are great, a hard worker, invaluable, etc., then this will peak the interest of the

---

30 Natalya Komarova, Telephone Interview, June 5, 2015

person you are trying to meet. For example, one of my mentors was previously inaccessible to me because I had no idea she existed but another one of my mentors made the connection for me and now she is in my network.

Who to network with?

It is important that we are pleasant with everyone we interact with because you never know who that person knows. As one interviewee puts it, "every interaction is a networking opportunity and a possibility to take my career to the next level."[31] A coworker of mine recently shared with me that she applied to a job in Washington, DC. The interviewer in Washington, DC knew an employee in our office and reached out to this employee to gather information about my coworker. My coworker had no idea that they knew each other and because she was always pleasant to this employee, the employee had

> **ACTION ITEM**
>
> **Be pleasant to everyone you meet because you never know who they know.**

---

31 Berry, Courtni, Telephone Interview, June 11, 2015

nothing negative to say about her. However, imagine if this employee had negative things to say about my coworker, this may have impacted her job and her reputation. You never know who knows who.

Where to network?

Networking is not only for the workplace but also for outside the workplace. Do not limit yourself. Inside the workplace, network with everyone and at a minimum, network with those at least one level above you. Interviewee, *Shontal Linder* recommends building a relationship with someone within the executive ranking who has influence in the decision making process.[32] This is extremely important because this person has some power and once you are able to build a relationship to where the person is committed to your growth, you have someone with influence in your corner. This person can plant the seeds for you and put in a good word. The higher ranked and more respected the person who is putting in the good word for you is, the more powerful that seed will be.

---

32 Linder, Shontal, Telephone Interview, June 25, 2015

CHAPTER 5:
STRATEGY 4: NETWORK! NETWORK! NETWORK!

The concept of planting a seed means that a thought is placed in someone's mind or brought to their attention that they may not act on immediately or use immediately, but it is left there in their subconscious until the right moment. In addition, a seed needs nourishment such as water to grow. The same applies to the informational seed that is planted; it needs validation, which can manifest in another seed by someone else, living up to the reputation, or seeing the person in action. While it may be more difficult to directly network with someone within the executive ranks, it is important that you network with people from all levels. Do not miss out on an opportunity because you assume the person cannot help you.

> *The help and blessing you need can come from anywhere, even the place you least expect it.*

Put yourself out there and in front of people you identify as a source of connection.

One avenue outside of work for networking is professional organizations. As a leader, I am a member of a handful of professional organizations that align with my career and life interests. Through these organizations, I have built strong relationships due to active participation and volunteering for events. The more I volunteer my time, the more people see me as an asset. Interviewee, *Carole Cimitile* recommended the following arenas:[33]

- American Society of Public Administration (ASPA) (national and/or local chapters)
- Local conferences such as Excellence in Government
- Alumni events
- Sororities
- Women in Government organization
- Google professional organizations in government or agency specialty
- Masters Degree Association such as Masters of Business Administration - MBA)
- Specialy in undergraduate school such Psi Chi for psychology majors

Interviewee, *Madonna Radcliff* recommend attending retirement parties[34] because you get to identify who is leaving and it provides the opportunity

---

33   Cimitile, Carole, Telephone Interview, June 29, 2015

34   Radcliff, Madonna, Telephone Interview, July 8, 2015

to network with a large group. However, what happens if there are no alumni or professional organization groups within your area? Then start one under a national organization if there is one.[35] This will allow you to network with the leaders of the national organization at a minimum and it will help you to build and practice your skills.

LinkedIn

A powerful tool, I highly recommended is LinkedIn. I have used LinkedIn for informational interviews, for internships, and for introductions to people who would be inaccessible. LinkedIn is a virtual networking site available 24/7. Search for people within a specific organization or your interest and connect with them. Instead of sending the scripted message LinkedIn drafts, I alter the message using the following format:

1. Give the person a compliment.
2. Point out something you both have in common.
3. Ask for help.
4. Say thank you.

---

35 McKee, Erin, Telephone Interview, June 30, 2015

It is human nature to enjoy hearing good things about ourselves; therefore, I always start with a compliment. Things I compliment range from how impressed I am with a person's job history or a specific task he/she did, or stating how highly he/she was recommended. I like to pull information from the person's LinkedIn profile so they know I spent time reading the information they spent time sharing on LinkedIn. This also shows the person respect and that I care. Second, pointing out something in common helps to close the distance and makes it easier for the person to relate to me. Third, it is also human nature to want to help others. Therefore, I ask for help and I am very specific regarding the help I am seeking. This allows the person to quickly identify how they can help and if they can. Lastly, I say thank you remaining polite and professional regardless of the outcome.

Therefore, in my introduction email, I have made the person feel good about themselves, built a connection, humbled myself by asking for help, and finished by being polite and saying thank you.

No matter where you network, never stop networking. One of my mentors warned me about this. She stated that the best time to network is when you don't need to network or when everything is just right in your life. Her logic was that you are not desperate for a connection, therefore, you can spend the time developing and building strong networks because sometimes the benefit of networking will take time.

> *When life is good, network and then network some more.*

How to network?

When networking always be yourself, smile, be friendly, and attentive. For in-person networking, it is highly recommended you do the following before ending a conversation:

- Find something both of you have in common.
- Discuss your assets such as skills, talents, and knowledge.
- Identify a potential need and how you can assist.
- Gather their contact information.

After meeting this person, send a follow-up message. In your email, remind them of what you had in common to help bring back a sense of connection, discuss how you may be of assistance, and always end by saying you look forward to remaining in contact. In addition, try to set up a time to meet in person or have a phone call. I do this within the first week while we can both recall our initial meeting.

> **ACTION ITEM**
>
> 1. Join LinkedIn, if you are already a member, then update your profile.
> 2. Grow you network by 1 person a day.
> 3. Give someone a compliment each day.

Another trick of mine is to take notes as soon as I walk away from the conversation or during the conversation depending on the flow of the conversation. I take notes to help me to remember who the person is, how I can help them, what I liked about them, and one thing unique to our conversation. My notes then help me to draft my follow-up email.

In addition, I find the person on LinkedIn if it was an in-person meeting and I continue to build the relationship. In my LinkedIn connection request, I identify when we met and one thing we discussed to jog the person's memory. Then I utilize the strategies mentioned above regarding how to network using LinkedIn. Interviewee, *Erin McKee* shared how she first identifies individuals with skills she wants to achieve, then she indicate to the person how much she admires something they did (lead a meeting, gave a speech, resolved a conflict) and acknowledges what she finds compelling.[36] This interviewee's strategies is based on building a relationship with a person, which is at the core of networking.

How to build an effective network?

- Don't always have your hand out, reach out to your network to share information and offer your assistance periodically; ***give don't always take***.
- Send articles pertaining to the person's business line or their interests.
- Invite the person out to other events such as a networking event or lunch.
- Continue to follow-up. The relationship shouldn't always be one-sided, continue to invest the time and maintain an open dialogue.

---

36 McKee, Erin, Telephone Interview, June 30, 2015

STRATEGY 5: FIND A SPONSOR

Purpose: Identify the difference between a mentor and a sponsor and the benefits of a sponsor.

The leaders I interviewed recommended having a sponsor, having more than one sponsor, and having an executive sponsor.

A sponsor is someone who will speak on your behalf when you are not around. For example: If an organization sponsors an event, they are putting their brand out there to support that event and to say to the world we are a part of this and we endorse it. The same applies to the sponsorship of people.

The difference between a sponsor and a mentor is that a mentor acts as a support tool as well as a source of advice whereas a sponsor is focused on building a protégé or boosting a career. Sponsors help you to get ahead and are much harder to acquire compared

CHAPTER 6:
STRATEGY 5: FIND A SPONSOR

to a mentor. They both require time, dedication, and focus. With sponsorship, your value or worth has to be demonstrated in order to capture the interest of the person providing the sponsorship. Think of any endorsement or sponsorship of any event. There is a mutually beneficial relationship that exists among the sponsor and the event personnel; the same holds true for career sponsors. It is important that you identify how you can help your sponsor because you will need a sponsor to open doors for you. A mentor can help to prepare and guide you for your next step but eventually, you will need a sponsor to put in that good word and bridge that connection. Some mentors will also act as sponsors but not all.

Some sponsors will be sought and some will arrive at your doorstep without any prior knowledge. Sometimes, sponsors will identify a person with great talents and begin to mold them. Some sponsors will be silent sponsors or investors. Similar to the financial world, silent investors are not present and may not be in the forefront but they are working hard in the background especially providing the necessary funds to advance. A silent sponsor operates in the same fashion for your career. They are present, speaking on your behalf, advocating for you without your knowledge and sometimes behind closed doors. Have you ever wondered how someone knows you or how you got selected or volun-told for a project – this is more likely than not, a silent sponsor who believed in you, recognized your talents and volunteered your services or networked for you.

No matter how you go about getting a sponsor, they are crucial to your career growth and advancement. In many organizations, sponsorship is the secret element for promotion. Get to know who management values, trusts, and listens to. Then get the attention of those people and build a positive relationship. A sponsor doesn't have to be asked. The key is to help them help you or scratch their backs so they can scratch yours. No matter which method you choose; building a valuable relationship, providing a helping hand or both, realize and understand you need help to advance. People listen to who they trust. Therefore, when a sponsor of yours is trusted among the leadership ranks starts speaking highly of you, people listen and take note. It is one thing if you try to brag about yourself but when someone else does it, it can

> **ACTION ITEM**
>
> **Get to know who management values, trusts, and listens to. Then build a relationship with that person.**

be received positively and taken as a consultation. The story I shared about my coworker who applied for a job in Washington, DC and the employee who spoke highly of her to the interviewer, is a perfect example of a sponsorship. You never know who can become your sponsor; therefore, treat everyone you interact with as a potential sponsor.

Who:

It is important to have someone in your immediate line of supervision become your sponsor, for example your direct supervisor. Your supervisor will more than likely be the one providing formal and informal references for you. Therefore, winning the sponsorship of your supervisor goes a long way. Executive sponsorship is also crucial because as you are looking to advance your career, the more sponsors you have in decision making ranks, the easier this growth becomes. Executive sponsors, often times have influence in the decision making process and can put in a good word for you.[37] Executive sponsors are also important because they provide networking opportunities and higher level/bigger picture outlook.

---

37   Linder, Shontal, Telephone Interview, June 25, 2015

Interviewee, *Madonna Radcliff* recommended having more than one sponsor and a diversity of sponsors. She shared a story how a co-worker of hers was tied to a rising star in the organization and as that person advanced, they took her coworker with them. However, when her agency went through major personnel change and the rising star left the company, her coworker was left stranded because he had tied his career and sponsorship needs to one person.[38] It is crucial that you acquire sponsors from different backgrounds and ranks within your agency. Co-workers are also a great sponsorship source because you never know who they know and how they may advance in their careers. You may be up for a position and a co-worker may have the power to plant a powerful seed.

How:

Before sponsorship can occur, it is important that you voice your goals and desires. Your supervisor cannot be your sponsor if they don't know what they are sponsoring. Make the job of sponsorship easy for your sponsor. Allow your work to speak for itself and build credibility in your office. One way to ***build credibility***

---

38   Radcliff, Madonna, Telephone Interview, July 8, 2015

CHAPTER 6:
STRATEGY 5: FIND A SPONSOR

is to do what you say and mean what you say. Make it easy for people to rely on you.

Two leaders discussed the strategy of sponsorship by stating that you should first voice your interests. For example, let your supervisor know that you are interested in a position particularly, management; make it clear that you want to volunteer for opportunities and that you want to advance your career. Don't assume that others know what you want, especially that you want to be promoted. Don't assume that your work will speak for itself and that others will notice your work and link it to your ambitions to advance your career.[39]

> *Use your voice, pair it with action, and remain consistent.*

(I've spoken about using your voice many times throughout this book because your voice is your power – you must use it and use it wisely).

At some point, ownership of your career comes back to you. Once you accept ownership, you can start

---

[39] Linder, Shontal, Telephone Interview, June 25, 2015; and Cimitile, Carole, Telephone Interview, June 29, 2015

to create a path for your career without relying on someone else to make your career happen. The help of others is necessary but you have still have to take the initiative and accept ownership.

One interviewee recommended volunteering for projects that management sponsors or getting into meetings where management is present. The main purpose is to get management and those in higher ranks to recognize your name, associate it with something positive and for them to get to know you (as a person, your values, your passion, and so forth).

STRATEGY 6: CONTROL YOUR EMOTIONS AND MANAGE YOUR STRESS

Purpose: Examine tactics and tips for stress management and properly addressing emotional concerns.

"Not everything that is faced can be changed, but nothing can be changed until it is faced."
– James Baldwin

It is imperative that we learn to master our emotions.

Many of the leaders I interviewed shared their thoughts on the importance of one's emotion and how to master those emotions.

Some of the recommendations I received from the interviewees include not taking things personally, learning to control your anger, finding ways to manage your stress outside of the office, not being easily ruffled, and not sharing too much of your personal information.[40]

Don't take things personally

Don't take things personally and don't let others see you take it personally. Don't change what got you where you are in your career.

When delivering bad news, I had to learn that the employee was going to be mad no matter what. I was on the receiving end of the employee's reaction because I delivered the news. Therefore, I had to learn not to take it personally. It is not an attack on us but on the decision made and as a leader, there will be decisions that some people will not like. Of course, it may be natural for us to initially feel a certain way or feel attacked, but what is important is that others do not see you taking it personally and that you do not dwell on it. It is okay to feel a certain way or have a personal reaction; absolutely vent when appropriate to someone you trust and then move on.

If you do not have the power to control the result, why take it personally and get yourself worked up over

---

40   Shabazz, Alia M, Telephone Interview, July 2, 2015

something. For example, you report to work and you're informed a specific report is due about your team and it is last minute. Why get worked up when you still have to do the report? Instead, vent and get your steam out but then shift your mindset and complete the report. Do it with a smile and show others that you can work under pressure.

In the process of not taking it personally, remain true to yourself and don't change what drove you to leadership in the first place. While others may try to change you, remember that your roots are important. One interviewee stated, to be successful, a leader cannot worry about what others think of them. She shared four key questions she asks herself when making a decision:

1 – Am I doing what I think is right?
2 – Will other people get upset with me?
3 – Can I live with others getting upset with me?
4 – Have I done the absolute best I can?[41]

If the answer to questions 1, 3, and 4 is no then a new solution is needed, however, if the answer to 1,

---

41 Interviewee A (anonymous), Telephone Interview, July 1, 2015

3, and 4 is yes, then stick with your decision and keep moving. Don't take it personally or be overly concerned with what others think of you. People will be upset with you but if you are comfortable, consistent, and stand by your decisions, then you're on the right track. Being consistent with the decisions you make helps to build trust with others.

> **ACTION ITEM**
>
> Before making a decision, ask yourself these four crucial questions:
> - 1 – Am I doing what I think is right?
> - 2 – Will other people get upset with me?
> - 3 – Can I live with others getting upset with me?
> - 4 – Have I done the absolute best I can?

Control your anger and other emotions

Controlling your anger and other emotions are very important to career success. Interviewee, *Alia M. Shabazz* shared how a professor told her class that they had to control their anger because there will be things in their career that will make them angry.[42] Reacting out of any emotion is hardly ever a good thing. It is always best to take a breather, walk away or sleep on it, and then react. Reacting out of anger, pain, sadness, or any other emotion may cause a regrettable action. In some agencies, some mistakes are harder to bounce back from. Therefore, minimize the incidents of mistakes by eliminating emotional outbursts.

Manage your stress

Finding ways to manage your stress outside the office is crucial to work life balance as well as your overall health. Interviewee, *Alia M. Shabazz*, explained how she wished she knew how to manage her stress early on and how to deal with stressful situations.[43] While we may want to be the best and say yes to everyone, we are no good to anyone if our health deteriorates. The care of yourself must be your #1 priority. There are numerous books, articles, and videos available that discusses different techniques to reduce stress. What works for me or the leaders I interviewed may not work for you. For example, some of the techniques I

---

42 Shabazz, Alia M, Telephone Interview, July 2, 2015

43 Ibid

use to reduce my stress include: having a strong faith in God and knowing he only gives me what I can handle, taking things one step at a time, breaking down a big task into smaller tasks, creating checklists, remaining organized, and having someone to talk to. On days that are really stressful, I may need to read a good book, have some good food, and watch a movie. No matter what works for you, what is more important is that you are aware of a proven method of alleviating your stress.

Another technique shared by interviewee, *Kaytura Felix* is to have fun and don't take yourself seriously.[44] Be able to laugh at your mistakes and keep it moving. This simple technique is a powerful one because not taking things to heart puts you in the right mindset, which we have discussed is a powerful strategy. Interviewee, *Kaytura Felix* goes on to encourage us to "take a deep breath, don't be so anxious about your career and life;…things will come;…calm down;…build your spirituality;…everything you want and more is already there."[45]

---

44   Felix, Kaytura, Telephone Interview, July 6, 2015

45   Ibid

Don't be easily ruffled

Not being easily ruffled is one piece of advice that I heard from more than one interviewee. The notion of having a poker face, not having people know what you are thinking by your facial expressions, or just having a certain demeanor was discussed. Interviewee, *Alia M. Shabazz* shared how there were times she interacted with people she found annoying but the person would never know because she remained cordial, kept a certain demeanor, and did not show her thoughts on her face.[46] For some, this is a difficult thing to do. Personally, I struggle with this because I find that showing certain emotions helps my employees relate better to me. However, I understand the power of such a demeanor. I have improved in this area by keeping a fluid awareness of my surroundings and who I am speaking with. At work, I am aware of those I can be more relaxed with and those who I cannot be so free with. These classifications have helped me tremendously however; I am cautious not to cross the line of showing favoritism. A technique to help with your demeanor or perception of your demeanor, is to stay above the fray, meaning do not get involved with gossip and hearsay. As a part of management being involved with gossip is frowned

---

46 Shabazz, Alia M, Telephone Interview, July 2, 2015

on and can hinder your advancement. Remain neutral, professional, and cordial.

Remain humble

Another factor of controlling your emotion, is to remain humble, stay focused on your goals, as well as do not let those who wish you ill will (aka. haters) get you down.[47] Being and remaining humble is a trait that some may struggle with but it allows you to be relatable to your peers and those you supervise. Humility is a trait respected by many. Showing your humility will show management that you are able to do all levels of work while remaining grateful.

Smile

No matter what you are doing, remember to smile.[48] Smiling goes a long way and it can work magic. Smiling is good for you and it helps those around you. A smile can help brighten your day, put you in a good frame of mind as well as do the same for the receiver (the person you are smiling at). Smiling helps put

---

47 McKee, Erin, Telephone Interview, June 30, 2015

48 Liddel, Emily, Telephone Interview, July 7, 2015

others at ease. A genuine smile can build trust, lighten the mood, and have others perceive you as a likable person. This is why I smile every time I meet someone and I try to always have a smile on face. Of course, there will be times when this will be more difficult but it is something I strive to do even through challenging times. Putting a smile on your face can help to lift the weight off your shoulders. Smiling and being nice to everyone you meet aligns with the strategies discussed thus far such as networking, mentoring, sponsorship, and having the right mindset.

Don't be afraid of your emotions

Do not be afraid of your emotions. We are gifted with certain emotions and capabilities for a reason. Women are categorized as intuitive and nurturing. Intuition is not a bad thing; it helps you to build stronger relationship because you are able to relate on a deeper level. It also helps you to sense what others may be truly thinking and feeling but are not voicing. These traits are gifts. Use them to build the career you want. As interviewee, *Emily Liddel* stated, "emotions and caring are not a bad thing…putting your heart into your employees is a good thing…it doesn't make you weak or emotional, it shows you care."[49] Men are also gifted with certain emotions that can be used as tools in their careers.

It all boils down to Emotional Intelligence.

---

49   Liddel, Emily, Telephone Interview, July 7, 2015

STRATEGY 7: SHOW INITIATIVE, VOLUNTEER, AND GO ABOVE & BEYOND

Purpose: Describe in detail how the small steps of showing initiative can have big results in advancing your career.

"Things may come to those who wait, but only things left by those who hustle."
– attributed to Abraham Lincoln

A key strategy that the leaders interviewed discussed was gaining exposure by volunteering for special assignments or projects, showing initiative, and having a can do attitude.

Interviewee, *Shontal Linder* shared how she gained her first leadership position by volunteering to take on a new work group that many in her office were not interested in. She accepted the challenge and in the end, the position gave her a chance to develop the work group, network, and learn new aspects of her job. [50]

By stepping up to the plate and taking on assignments others find difficult or unattractive, you position yourself to grow your network and build crucial skills important to your agency. Interviewee, *Carole Cimitile* shared how her willingness to step up to the plate provided her with the opportunity to interact with individuals in leadership at her office.[51] Special assignments help to demonstrate to others your potential and value. If there are any doubts about your capabilities, successfully delivering on a special project or assignment goes a long way to quiet those doubts. In addition, if you volunteer for an opportunity, it is crucial that you see it as such – an opportunity. The task is important to someone out there, that is why it is a special assignment, and you never know who is watching these assignments. It is very difficult to predict exactly what new opportunities will follow. Therefore, always remain open to opportunities especially those that can offer you new experiences. Have a can do attitude and it will take you very far.

---

50   Linder, Shontal, Telephone Interview, June 25, 2015

51   Cimitile, Carole, Telephone Interview, June 29, 2015

CHAPTER 8: STRATEGY 7:
SHOW INITIATIVE, VOLUNTEER, & GO ABOVE & BEYOND

When you volunteer for outreach activities or work assignments, this helps you to be visible and remain visible. Once you begin to do this more than once, people will begin to depend on you. You will be associated or known as the person who is willing to go above and beyond, volunteer, and is not afraid of the unknown. Once you volunteer for one special project, it opens the door for other special projects. It is important that I mention again that for each project, be mindful that you never know who is watching; therefore, consistently produce at a level that makes you and others proud. No job is too small or big for you to do. Give everything your best effort because:[52]

> *"When you can be trusted with the small things; you can be trusted with the big things."*

Upon consistently delivering a high caliber of work, your work will begin to stand out and speak for itself. At this point, you are creating a reputation for yourself. Some of the leaders I interviewed shared how

---

52 Liddel, Emily, Telephone Interview, July 7, 2015

they were promoted based off of the special projects they worked on.

You do not have to only seek volunteer activities or special assignments within your agency. You can offer your services to your community. There are many ways to find things to volunteer for. You can go through your church, local community center, conduct an online search, word of mouth, professional organizations, or by using LinkedIn. To find ways to spend your time as an intern or as a volunteer on LinkedIn, utilize the tactics identified in the prior chapters. You can connect with a person or an organization on LinkedIn.

Volunteering outside of work allows you to give back to the community, spend your energy on a cause that is important to you, and develop your skillsets. Seek out leadership positions in the community that you think you may not be ready for or may be high risk because the fear of losing your income will not be a factor.[53] Often times, high risk positions will push you to new heights you never imagined. The knowledge you gain (whether the results are good or bad) will be valuable. Remember, the experiences you gain

---

53 Interviewee A (anonymous), Telephone Interview, July 1, 2015

from your volunteer activities are a resume booster.

> **ACTION ITEM**
>
> 1. Seek out projects within your agency and volunteer for them. Pay particular attention to cutting edge projects because these will have the attention of executive level leaders. Your goal should be to volunteer for at least one activity every year.
> 2. Take the initiative to identify a problem and a solution. Own and deliver the solution. Look for the little things that no one is thinking about.

Quick Tips:

1. Be intentional about exposing yourself to various opportunities within your agency.[54]

    a) This tip was shared by interviewee, *Courtni Berry*, who explained that she is intentional in the opportunities she takes on because

---

54   Berry, Courtni, Telephone Interview, June 11, 2015

she wants to become well versed in multiple subjects.

b) This is important to consider because not all opportunities are the right fit. Sometimes, you will need a mentor or a network connection to help decipher an opportunity. For example, I had the opportunity to become a trainer for my agency but I was advised by one of my mentors that it wasn't the right fit. It was a hard pill to swallow but I listened and other opportunities presented themselves that were a better fit. In addition, some positions may be dead end positions, and you may not know that without having a mentor, sponsor, or friend to advise you.

2. Anticipate the needs of your office and/or agency.[55]

a) Identifying the needs of the agency may arise from your own observations but it can also arise from you asking a simple question – *what can I do for you?* You may also state,

---

55   Liddel, Emily, Telephone Interview, July 7, 2015

I notice you need (fill in the blank), let me assist.[56] Do not wait for people to ask you to do something, make the offer to do it.

b) No matter how small a problem or solution, discuss it with management with the goal of implementing it. This will demonstrate to management that you are invested in the office and agency and that you add value by providing solutions and improvements. As a leader, this is a powerful skill but it can also be implemented as a non-management level employee. Share your ideas with your supervisor and inform him/her that you are willing to develop the solution on your own personal time if necessary. By volunteering to take ownership and do the work, this shows you are self-sufficient and solidifies your capabilities as a leader.

3. Take on things that stretch you beyond what you think you can do.[57]

a) Remember the chapters discussing fear

---

56   Shane, Glynnis, Telephone Interview, June 26, 2015

57   Liddel, Emily, Telephone Interview, July 7, 2015

and mindset. Fear is the greatest thing that can hold you back. I recognize that this is difficult to do but it is necessary. Push yourself, make strides to overcome those fears, and do your best. These projects that you volunteer for are important to somebody but they are also important for you. They give you something new and/or different to do, provide you with new skill(s), helps others to see you in a different perspective, and puts you on the radar of influential people.

4. Identify the key resources within your agency.[58] Figure out who is responsible for what and learn as much from them as possible. Therefore, if and when a problem arises, you will know how to assist or who to go to. Also, build relationships with key individuals because there will come a time when you will need to rely on their services. Building strong relationships will assist in any favors you may need.

5. Sometimes, an assignment may be a lateral

---

58 Shane, Glynnis, Telephone Interview, June 26, 2015

CHAPTER 8: STRATEGY 7:
SHOW INITIATIVE, VOLUNTEER, & GO ABOVE & BEYOND

move,[59] do not shy away from these if they have the potential for upgrade down the line. Do not dismiss an assignment just on face value, dig a little deeper.

6. Sometimes, certain projects may not request your assistance.[60] However, once you become aware that a special project or assignment is in the works, identify who is in charge, and contact that person to offer your assistance. Do not wait, show that you are in-tune and aware of the events happening within your agency, and that you are not afraid to put yourself out there. Sometimes, you may be overlooked because the deciding official may not know you are interested or you may not be on their short list of people they desire. It is your job, as a new or seasoned leader, to be on the deciding official's short list. To do so, you may have to toot your own horn.

7. Sharing is caring.[61] Share your knowledge. If you identify that others are struggling or need

---

59 Radcliff, Madonna, Telephone Interview, July 8, 2015

60 Ibid

61 Zimmerman, Ruth, Telephone Interview, July 6, 2015

help, be that helping hand. ***People remember those who were willing to help when they didn't have to.*** However, depending on your agency, not everything is shareable. It is important to find a mentor but it is also just as important for you to become a mentor too. Lending a helpful hand doesn't have to turn into mentoring, but you should not shy away from it, if it does.

Sample Ideas:

The following ideas were recommended by the interviewees.

1. I have implemented the following idea in my office by obtaining buy-in from management and employees.

    a) <u>*The idea*</u>: Create a website that houses all the details and special projects available to employees and managers in your office.[62]

    b) <u>*What I did*</u>: In my agency, there are a lot of leadership programs locally and nationally that most employees are unaware of.

---

62 Shane, Glynnis, Telephone Interview, June 26, 2015

In addition, most employees feel that management has little interest in their development. Therefore, I identified the problem for managers and employees. Next, I presented this idea to key personnel in management and discussed the benefit for employees and management. In addition, I offered to create the site as well as manage it. Once I received the stamp of approval, I began making presentations to employees in small groups to market the new site. This was a successful project and I was able to add value as a supervisor and solve a problem.

2. Find free training classes and put a list together.[63] The training topics could be whatever your agency requires. For example, if learning about how to manage and lead a virtual team is necessary for your agency, find a free training that managers can attend or participate virtually. To get buy-in remember to speak in terms of how it benefits the audience and sell it as if they thought of the idea.

---

63 Shane, Glynnis, Telephone Interview, June 26, 2015

a) If management is not willing or able to attend the session, negotiate that you attend, gather the information, and then train on the information learned. Once again, you solidify yourself as an asset and become a subject matter expert on the topic.

3. Create an agenda when you are meeting with someone, listing the talking points you want to discuss.[64]

   a) This tip was shared by interviewee, *Alia M. Shabazz*. She shared how this tip helped to impress leaders within her agency.

   b) This technique shows you are prepared, organized, and goes above and beyond. This will assist in a building a certain reputation.

4. Volunteer to be the organizer of a charity event. Volunteer for special projects, such as a charity campaign.[65] This gives you an opportunity to sharpen and showcase your skills outside of

---

64 Shabazz, Alia M, Telephone Interview, July 2, 2015

65 McNabb, JoAnne, Telephone Interview, June 25, 2015

CHAPTER 8: STRATEGY 7:
SHOW INITIATIVE, VOLUNTEER, & GO ABOVE & BEYOND

your regular duties. You will also broaden your network of colleagues, to potentially include executives. If your office has an annual charity event, then get on board. If not, task yourself with helping your agency to do more charity work. Do the research necessary and connect with other agencies for advice if necessary.

5. Volunteer to take notes at meetings or to write reports of decisions made. Good writers are not easy to find in most organizations. If you are one, look for chances to demonstrate it.[66] For example, if you are already in leadership, volunteer to do this for a meeting that is important to your supervisors. In my agency, we put out local policy via written directives and all managers are required to attend bi-weekly staff meetings. These are two areas that may be the same or similar in your agency that may offer the opportunity for initiative.

    a) This may seem to be a daunting task, which will cause many people to shy away from it. Taking notes or writing a memo allows you to be in charge of defining what occurred

---

66   McNabb, JoAnne, Telephone Interview, June 25, 2015

or should occur. You have the ability to shape or mold the document as you see fit.

6. If your agency offers research programs or assignments, volunteer for them.

The will to take the initiative, lies with being motivated. Motivation for some comes easy and for others, not so much. No matter what the instance, motivation is necessary to go above and beyond.

> *Motivation is the fuel and key ingredient to do more.*

STRATEGY 8: BE PREPARED AND REMAIN PREPARED

Purpose: In prior chapters, I discussed the power and necessity of networking, sponsorship, and mentoring. These elements are crucial parts of being prepared and remaining prepared. In this chapter, I will discuss a few more elements to help you become prepared for leadership roles and remain prepared and ready.

> "The will to win is worthless if you do not have the will to prepare."
> – Thane Yost

> "It is not often that a man can make opportunities for himself. But he can put himself in such shape that when or if the opportunities come he is ready."
> --Theodore Roosevelt

***P**reparation and practice are crucial for success.*

You should never be in a position where you feel as if you know it all because someone is always out to get your job. The goal in any leadership role is to be the best and remain the best. To become the best, it takes work, motivation, practice, and support. No leader is able to do it on their own.

I received an abundance of advice on this topic from the leaders I interviewed. They all spoke strongly about the importance of preparation on their career.

In my career, I have practiced the art of preparation. Most times I am unsure what I am preparing for but I am aware of where I want to be because I made goals. Based on my goals, I take the necessary steps to get me to my next career point. Therefore, when I wanted a career in leadership, I read books, sought out leadership programs, sought out mentors who were leaders, and gained experiences to help me practice my leadership abilities. I continued to hone in my skills until I landed my first leadership role. Now I am in the works of preparing for my next leadership role, which will entail more responsibility. My preparation led me from obtaining my first leadership role and a promotion all within the span of writing this book (approximately seven months).

Preparation includes:

1. Leadership programs
2. Workshops/Lectures
3. Education (Degree/Certificate)
4. Mentors
5. Networking
6. Books
7. Professional Organizations
8. Trade magazines/journals
9. Understanding expectations
10. Answering - What does the next level look like?
11. Answering - Who are my competitors?
12. Remaining technically competent

To remain prepared, it is important to pay close attention and remain engaged. Do not disengage yourself. Keep abreast of the social perception of yourself, your agency, and your position. Remain in-tune with your agency's structure[67] and personnel changes. Who is retiring, where is there an upcoming personnel need, who needs assistance? Knowing information regarding your agency future projections and goals can help you to market certain skillsets and buzzwords. For example, my agency is transitioning to an electronic

---

67   McKee, Erin, Telephone Interview, June 30, 2015

environment. Trainings are being conducted via Microsoft Lync instant message/conferencing tool. Originally, this tool had limited users in my office. I saw this as an opportunity and became an expert on this tool. As more and more training was required to be held thru Lync, my knowledge and technical expertise became valuable.

A **mentor** can also be a valuable tool to help you prepare and remain prepared. As mentioned earlier, a mentor can assist in your understanding of the work culture and any nuisances within the agency, especially landmines.[68] As you advance your career, the work culture and unspoken rules become more and more important; having someone to guide you through the dos and don'ts (landmines) is an invaluable asset. For example, having a mentor steer you away from a particular job because it is frowned upon in your agency or is a dead-end, saves you a lot of time and heartache.

Knowledge is a major preparation activity. It entails the formal education process (school), lectures, workshops, and literatures/books.

---

68 McKee, Erin, Telephone Interview, June 30, 2015

CHAPTER 9:
STRATEGY 8: BE PREPARED AND REMAIN PREPARED

> *"In order to remain competitive, one must continually maintain a level of expertise both academically and professionally in their chosen profession."* [69]

Interviewee, *Carolyn McMillon* shared how obtaining her master's degree was essential for her to break into upper management. She explained that at this level, almost everyone competing for the next promotion is competent and qualified; therefore, you have to find ways to shine. Education can be used as a screen-out element; therefore, if you lack the necessary education level you could be eliminated from the competitive process. She shared that every good leader is looking for someone who is continuously developing themselves and strives to remain in a state of continuous development.[70] Seek out opportunities with other teams in order to gain exposure and learn something new.

---

69 McMillon, Carolyn, Telephone and email interview, June 8 & 19, 2015

70 Ibid

Get to know who the knowledgeable people are within your agency and learn from them.[71] Relationship is the key to great success especially as a leader. Therefore, identify the knowledgeable individuals and align yourself with them. Spend time consulting with other leaders and seek their advice.[72] As I shared before, people love to help and give advice as long as they do not fear competition; capitalize on this and work it to your advancement. Open up the conversation asking for help.

Books are another great source of information. Some of the leaders I interviewed shared some of the books that helped them in their journey of career success and advancement. These include:

- *Fierce Conversation* - Susan Scott
- *It Worked for Me: In Life and Leadership* – Colin Powell
- *Lean In: Women, Work, and the Will to Lead* – Sheryl Sandberg
- *How to Become CEO: The Rules for Rising to the Top of Any Organization* – Jeffrey Fox

---

71 Linder, Shontal, Telephone Interview, June 25, 2015

72 McMillon, Carolyn, Telephone and email interview, June 8 & 19, 2015

CHAPTER 9:
STRATEGY 8: BE PREPARED AND REMAIN PREPARED

- *Good to Great Collections* – Jim Collins
- *The Success Principles* – Jack Canfield and Janet Switzer
- *Putting Things First* – Stephen Covey, A. Roger Merrill, and Rebecca R. Merrill
- *The Effective Executive* - Peter Drucker
- *The 7 Habits of Highly Effective People* – Stephen R. Covey
- *Nice Girls Don't Get the Corner Office* – Lois P. Frankel
- *The Well-Spoken Woman: Your Guide to Looking and Sounding Your Best* – Christine K. Jahnke
- *Creating Personal Presence: Look, Talk, Think, and Act Like a Leader* – Dianna Boohner
- Harvard Business Review

Interviewee, *Carolyn McMillon* recommends remaining technically competent by staying abreast on leadership strategies because our skills are perishable, they can become outdated. She recommends reviewing various recruiting sites (federal and private sector) to determine what skills employers are looking for and how your field may be changing. She also recommends looking at the biographies of the leaders in your field to determine if you are still competent in your field.[73]

---

73 McMillon, Carolyn, Telephone and email interview, June 8 & 19, 2015

> **ACTION ITEM**
>
> Subscribe to journals and professional organizations specific to your field; attend conferences and workshops. These avenues will help you to identify trends and changes for your field.

In some agencies, the **expectations others have** of you, as a leader, may be skewed; identify what these expectations are and either live up to that expectation or outshine them. Gathering this type of knowledge will help you identify the threats you face, your competitors, and your supporters.

Within your agency, **watch how leaders interact with each other**; this can help you identify how to interact with those leaders and others. It can also help you to identify any interaction mishaps and assist in mastering your own skills and talents. Imitating others you identify with is also a means of preparation. Interviewee, *Alia M. Shabazz* recommends mimicking and modeling the behaviors that resonate with you.[74]

---

[74] Shabazz, Alia M, Telephone Interview, July 2, 2015

Interviewee, *Courtni Berry* also recommends shadowing leaders you think you can learn from.[75]

Leadership programs:

For my career and agency, leadership programs are crucial for career advancement. Before I was in my first leadership role I was a part of a leadership program. It was a major resume booster as well as an informative process. I was able to enhance my toolbox and once I obtained my first leadership role, I was able to put the tools I had to use. This leadership program also taught me about my agency (gave me a mission level perspective) and provided an opportunity to network. I was able to learn more about my agency, which would not have been possible without the leadership program.

As a leader, I still partake in leadership programs. I am currently involved in a leadership program, which is very prestigious in my agency and has the capability to put me on the fast track for career advancement and on the list of leaders for my agency to choose from. Identify programs within your own organization that are highly respected. Once you identify such

---

75   Berry, Courtni, Telephone Interview, June 11, 2015

program(s), look at the application process and prepare yourself for applying if you do not already qualify. I have learned that sometimes, certain programs are not advertised within the organization, therefore, you have to find these programs by researching and advocating for the program. If anything, ask for help from your mentor and keep your mind and interest on these programs as you network. Lastly, the leadership programs do not have to take place at your job; it could be in your community. Interviewee, *Carolyn McMillon*, shared how she learned different leadership strategies and how to best deal with leadership challenges through leadership programs within her agency and in her community.[76]

Not only are leadership programs a great tool but so are *developmental opportunities*. These may take form as a leadership program but sometimes, it may be a special project or assignment. Development opportunities are just that – opportunities to help develop you as a person and/or leader. Seek them out and do not shy away from them; they will improve your capabilities and experiences.

---

76 McMillon, Carolyn, Telephone and email interview, June 8 & 19, 2015

CHAPTER 9:
STRATEGY 8: BE PREPARED AND REMAIN PREPARED

Quick items:

1. As previously mentioned, prepare an agenda for any meeting you are conducting. Do the background research and know the details.[77]

2. Set clear and concise goals that are true to you. Set goals that are attainable and goals that will challenge you.[78] Seek buy-in from your supervisor.

3. The following are recommendations provided by interviewee, *Madonna Radcliff*.[79]

    a. Learn the work culture, the circles/cliques, and the language. Learn how to break into these circles. People hire who they know and like. Therefore, become known and liked in your agency.

        i. To do this, talk to people, be friendly, be true to yourself, observe, and listen. Have a goal in mind and understand

---

77 Shabazz, Alia M, Telephone Interview, July 2, 2015

78 Cimitile, Carole, Telephone Interview, June 29, 2015

79 Radcliff, Madonna, Telephone Interview, July 8, 2015

that certain things take time.

b. Develop your interview skills because you can use interviews to showcase your skills, gain sponsors, and network.

   i. She shared how she went on interviews and with preparation (interview books, research, learning who is on the interview panel) and practice, she knocked it out the park. As a result, the interviewers identified that she could interview, learned about her background, and were impressed. From this experience she has had a Chief Administrative Officer (CAO) of an agency reach out to her a couple of imes in an attempt to get her to work for him. Therefore, even if you don't get the job, some of the interviewers, especially the senior individuals will remember how much they really like you when another opening becomes available.

c. Identify promotional opportunities that you qualify for and seek them out. If these

CHAPTER 9:
STRATEGY 8: BE PREPARED AND REMAIN PREPARED

positions are being held, learn when the person holding the position will retire.

d. Set up a meeting with the top executives in your agency. At this meeting, ask them what skills or experiences you need and then seek out the opportunity to gain those skill(s) and/or experience(s). This way any perceived barriers are removed.

4. Take the Myers Briggs Assessment and DISC Assessment, so you can learn how you react to different situations and how others may perceive you based on your reactions. The more you know about yourself, the more you can adjust your behavior to make sure you are well perceived.[80]

5. Speak with leaders and learn their strategies and obstacles.[81] This will help you to know that some of the challenges you have faced are not specific to you. It provides the opportunity to learn from leaders who have experienced the journey, which is what I hope this book has

---

80 Zimmerman, Ruth, Telephone Interview, July 6, 2015

81 Komarova, Natalya, Telephone interview, June 5, 2015

done for you so far.

Recently, I was down because I was dealing with certain challenges on my team. I thought maybe I was doing something wrong but after speaking with another leader, she confirmed she would have made the same decisions in my shoes. This provided tremendous relief and confirmation that I was on the right track. There will be days where this type of reassurance is needed.

It is important that you remind yourselve that *"there is no growth in the comfort zone and no comfort in the growth zone."* [82]

Growth is crucial to your development and advancement as a leader; therefore, stepping out your comfort zone should be practiced often. You will be surprise what you can learn and what you may end up liking and excelling at. Never miss an opportunity because you are uncomfortable. I dislike conflicts at work, whether that is voicing my opinions that are different from my supervisor or delivering negative news. Recently, I held an emergency meeting with my team because I sensed they were stressed. I called this

---

82 McMillon, Carolyn, Telephone and email interview, June 8 & 19, 2015

CHAPTER 9:
STRATEGY 8: BE PREPARED AND REMAIN PREPARED

meeting with the expectation that I may not like the feedback I hear. This was very uncomfortable for me and I would have preferred to avoid holding the meeting but it was necessary. I invited the union president to the meeting in order to help my employees be brutally honest without fear of reprimand. As expected, they were brutally honest and they were able to get a lot of things off their chest. As a result of this meeting, my employees developed additional respect for me because they realized I put myself in the crossfire to hear them out. As I work through the challenges my team voiced, I am confident that the meeting, while it made me uncomfortable, provided a solid foundation and necessary growth.

STRATEGY 9: REPUTATION AND PERCEPTION

Purpose: To identify the power of a good reputation and to explore the idea that the perception others have of you is their reality of you. This chapter also discusses how to develop a good reputation.

"Character is like a tree and reputation like a shadow.
The shadow is what we think of it; the
ttree is the real thing."
– Abraham Lincoln

Perception is reality.

I live by this fact because no matter what your personal truth is, what people perceive of you will dictate their reality of you. If people perceive you as a dictator, while you consider yourself to just

> **ACTION ITEM**
>
> 1. Create a positive reputation and protect it.
> 2. Be aware of your reputation.

CHAPTER 10:
STRATEGY 9: REPUTATION AND PERCEPTION

follow the rules, the reality will be that you are a dictator. Therefore, it is paramount that you create a positive reputation and protect it. People will react to you based on your reputation and it can open or close doors. Be aware of your reputation and the perception people have of you.

Having a good reputation is a work of art. It puts people at ease and builds trust. To build trust, you have to be able to meet the perception people have of you. You may be wondering, how you can know how people perceive you and what your reputation is. The answer is to ask for feedback. Sometimes, people will provide this information to you, but if they don't, just ask. Don't be afraid! The feedback you hear may be shocking but ***dig deep and don't react; just listen***. Ask questions to identify why people perceive you the way they do. Even if you disagree, try to pinpoint which behavior reinforces the perception they have. Try to identify the true/real message. For example, I had an employee tell me that they feel I don't listen. I found this shocking because I always considered myself a good listener, however, the employee perceived me as a horrible listener because I gave generic responses such as "I hear you." After making that statement, the employee stated I would move on to the next topic, which made them feel as if I wasn't listening. Of course, this stems from certain conversations but I have learned that summarizing what someone says to me, giving an immediate response, or following up with a response makes the employee feel as if he/she is being heard. In the end, my employee just wanted to know that her thoughts matters.

There are certain characteristics or reputations managers like to work with. These include hard worker, knowledgeable, easy to work with, professional, reliable, credible, high quality of work, initiator, and honest. Many of the leaders I interviewed discussed how their reputation and the perception others had of them assisted in their career advancement. Interviewee, *Alia M. Shabazz* shared how her colleagues and leaders within her agency recommended her for leadership roles and projects. She stated that she built credibility by understanding the policy of her agency, speaking to the issues, and providing good customer service.[83] In my office, I have a very strong reputation of being knowledgeable. Every now and then, I am amazed how strong this reputation is because the technical knowledge that created this reputation is no longer my job function but people remember my aptitude; I left an imprint and it stuck. This reputation has helped

---

83 Shabazz, Alia M, Telephone Interview, July 2, 2015

CHAPTER 10:
STRATEGY 9: REPUTATION AND PERCEPTION

me to get into management because there is a need for managers with technical expertise and my reputation made it to the hiring manager's ears and caught her attention. Let your work validate your reputation.

A strong reputation that travels from department to department and stands the test of time requires consistency. If you wish to have a reputation of high quality work, then it is not good enough to produce high quality work once, it is necessary to do it every single time. ***You never know when your work will impress someone.*** Interviewee, *Alia M. Shabazz* stated that there is always someone watching you.[84] You will never know who those people are but as long as you keep this concept in your thoughts, you will be okay. Since people talk and you don't know who they know, it is a good idea to always carry yourself in a manner that you will be proud of. As mentioned earlier, you should carry yourself in a manner that your supervisor does not have to worry about what you are doing.[85] Build a level of trust where people do not have to question you.

Interviewee, *Carolyn McMillon* stated, our reputations precede us and oftentimes people can see

---

84   Shabazz, Alia M, Telephone Interview, July 2, 2015

85   Ibid.

you coming long before you reach them.[86] Therefore, establish yourself as a trustworthy person with integrity, that way, your boss will know they can give you an assignment and it will come in accurate and on time. When you say you are going to deliver on something, then deliver, if not, provide guidance or an update in advance. This ties into your character of being reliable and trust-worthy.

Other items mentioned by the interviewees include:

1. If you complain, provide solutions.[87]

    a. By demonstrating you are a person who brings solutions to the table, this makes you very valuable in the eyes of your supervisors and those in higher ranks. Being able to provide effective solutions and gather buy-in is a crucial skill any leader should have.

2. When you make a mistake, own up to it.[88]

---

86 McMillon, Carolyn, Telephone and email interview, June 8 & 19, 2015

87 Liddel, Emily, Telephone Interview, July 7, 2015

88 Zimmerman, Ruth, Telephone Interview, July 6, 2015

STRATEGY 10: APPLY & DO IT

Purpose: Get the courage and just do it! Apply! Apply! And Apply!

"Inaction breeds doubt and fear. Action breeds confidence and courage. If you want to conquer fear, do not sit home and think about it, go out and get busy."
– Dale Carnegie

Inaction is the root of failure.

Do not let fear hold you back. Throughout this book, I discussed the power of having the right mindset, getting out of your comfort zone, and the consequences of remaining stuck inside of fear. ***All the strategies discussed mean nothing unless you apply***

ACTION ITEM

Go on a job interview for a job you do not want and have a good interview.

them. Take the bits and pieces of information shared here that apply to you and put them to work. When you do it, remember to remain flexible, be open, and stay positive. The best time to apply for a job is when you don't need one. Imagine, going on an interview and not having the stress of needing the job. Imagine how at ease you would feel to know that your income doesn't rest in the interviewer's hand. Imagine the power you will feel to know that you are doing this interview to sharpen your interview skills and test the waters. WOW! What a feeling! Don't wait until there is a need, do it on your time and enjoy the ride. This is a valuable learning opportunity.

A common concept among the leaders I interviewed focused on the concept of actively pursuing your career, being in control, and just doing what needs to be done. Interviewee, *Courtni Berry* stated, "you have responsibility over your own career, don't depend on your supervisor to promote you; take action for yourself."[89] The same applies for the strategies discussed in this book. The power to make your dreams a reality and to advance your career lies within you. It takes hard work, dedication, focus, and drive, but you can do it.

---

89 Berry, Courtni, Telephone Interview, June 11, 2015

CHAPTER 11:
STRATEGY 10: APPLY & DO IT

When you are considering where or what to apply for be flexible and open to different possibilities. Another common theme I heard during the interviews was to be open to moving around within your agency, to different agencies, and moving to different locations (city, state, or country). One interviewee recommended working at different agencies in order to gain a new perspective.[90] When you are willing to move around, it opens up the possibility to acquire new skills and expand your network. Be willing to move to different locations. This may not be ideal due to the logistics involved in moving, but if you are able to move around (different states) it increases your ability to advance your career on the fast track. Interviewee, *Carolyn McMillon* shared how she passed her peers that started with her in her agency because she was willing to move around and take on jobs no one was willing to do. She stated:[91]

> *"career mobility is advantageous for career progression."*

---

90 Radcliff, Madonna, Telephone Interview, July 8, 2015

91 McMillon, Carolyn, Telephone and email interview, June 8 & 19, 2015

Applying outside of your organization also presents the opportunity to move up the pay scale faster compared to staying within your organization. Interviewee, *Glynnis Shane* explains:

> "be patient, sometimes it's easier to get promoted outside than inside; if you can't get promoted then look outside…you're only stuck if you say you're stuck."[92]

Other tips I learned from the leaders I interviewed are as follows:

- Identify what is important to you and find an organization that is a fit. Remember work life balance. All work and no play will not make you happy and successful in the long run.

- Don't forget to regularly update your resume and look at your knowledge, skills, and abilities (KSA).[93]

    o It is a good idea to make a running list describing all the projects and positions

---

92 Shane, Glynnis, Telephone Interview, June 26, 2015

93 Radcliff, Madonna, Telephone Interview, July 8, 2015

CHAPTER 11:
STRATEGY 10: APPLY & DO IT

you've held throughout your career. As you take on new projects and job roles, you can update this document and it serves as a tool for your interview and resume. This has worked tremendously for me.

- When you apply for a job, ensure that your resume identify all the key tasks or words listed in the job posting. These key words can be found in the description, duties, and KSA sections. One clue to identify if a task or word is important is whether or not it appears numerous times throughout the job posting.

Remember, your career is your own. Put in the work, be deliberate, and passionate about all your actions. The strategies discussed are here to aide you in your journey of growth, change, success, and most of all career advancement.

TIPS FOR LEADERS

Purpose: In this chapter, I will highlight some powerful quotes I collected as part of the development process for this book as well as advice the leaders wanted me to share with you, the reader.

Quotes:

"Resist your fear; fear will never lead you to a positive end."
— T.D Jakes

"Thinking is easy, acting is difficult, and to put one's thoughts into action is the most difficult thing in the world."
— Johann Wolfgang von Goethe

"Folks who never do any more than they get paid for, never get paid for any more than they do."
— Elbert Hubbard

"Even if you are on the right track, you'll get run over if you just sit there."
— Will Rogers

CHAPTER 12:
TIPS FOR LEADERS

"Don't wait for your ship to come in, swim out to it."
— Cathy Hopkins

"Motivation is the fuel necessary to keep the human engine running."
— Zig Ziglar

"[Women] must pay for everything.... They do get more glory than men for comparable feats. But, also, women get more notoriety when they crash."
—Amelia Earhart

"You can make more friends in two months by becoming interested in other people than you can in two years by trying to get other people interested in you."
— Dale Carnegie

"Networking is marketing. Marketing yourself, marketing your uniqueness, marketing what you stand for."
— Christine Comaford-Lynch

"A mentor is someone who sees more talent and ability within you, than you see in yourself, and helps bring it out of you."
—Bob Proctor

"The delicate balance of mentoring someone is not creating them in your own image, but giving them the opportunity to create themselves."
—Steven Spielberg

"Mentoring is a brain to pick, an ear to listen, and a push in the right direction."
— John C. Crosby

More Advice and quotes from the leaders I interviewed:

Carolyn McMillon [94]
- The # 1 test of being a good leader is seeing if people are willing to follow you voluntarily.
- Leadership is not steady; it fluctuates.
- Leaders have to be willing to pull employees up.
- Don't be afraid to say, "I don't know" but always follow with "I will find out."
- The challenge is to work with people in such a way that they will voluntarily give you their discretionary effort.

---

94   McMillon, Carolyn, Telephone and email interview, July 8 & 19, 2015

CHAPTER 12:
TIPS FOR LEADERS

Interviewee A[95]

- Treat others with respect – people don't hire people they don't like or respect (treat all you interact with respect).
- She quoted, "people are either an example or a warning."
- Learn to have difficult conversations. Sometimes all people want is to be heard and to know that they are being taken seriously. Truly listen to your employees.
  - This is a crucial skill to have. If this is not one of your skills, I recommend finding a career coach, reading a book on this topic, taking courses, asking your mentor, or finding someone that exceeds in this area and soliciting for their help.

Alia M. Shabazz [96]

- Handle difficult changes by knowing your job; be upfront with people, the longer you withhold information, the worse it becomes because it is what it is.
- Don't cross a line that cannot be crossed back,

---

[95] Interviewee A (anonymous), Telephone Interview, July 1, 2015

[96] Shabazz, Alia M, Telephone Interview, July 2, 2015

especially in the gray areas. People will try you but you cannot be ignorant of the law.
- When giving feedback, give it in a spirit of wanting the team to be better.

Carole Cimitile [97]
- Resources for women leaders
    - List of best places to work for women
    - *Working women* magazine
    - Partnership for Public Service
    - Senior Executive Association
    - MSPB – Merit System Protection Board
    - OPM.gov
    - Women in Government Association

Emily Liddel [98]
- Pull back from socializing because you do not want to be perceived as showing special treatment.
- Plan events with your entire working unit/team.

---

97 Cimitile, Carole, Telephone Interview, June 29, 2015

98 Liddel, Emily, Telephone Interview, July 7, 2015

CHAPTER 12:
TIPS FOR LEADERS

Ruth Zimmerman[99]

- Say good morning to everyone every day.
- For every email you send, try to call as much as you can.
- Show your employees that you care, that you listen, and that you are invested in them.
- Learn the little things about your employees that are important to them. Remember what your employees tell you and occasionally bring it up because when you do, your employees will be surprised that you remembered. For example, remembering their favorite meal. Get curious, ask questions, and listen; dig deep with your questions so you can get a better understanding of your team.

Erin McKee [100]

- Take care of your team.
- Think about the mission and goals of your agency and keep an eye on delivering them.

---

99   Zimmerman, Ruth, Telephone Interview, July 6, 2015

100 McKee, Erin, Telephone Interview, June 30, 2015

BIBLIOGRAPHY

Leaders Interviewed

Berry, Courtni, Telephone Interview, June 11, 2015

Cimitile, Carole, Telephone Interview, June 29, 2015

Felix, Kaytura, Telephone Interview, July 6, 2015

Interviewee A (anonymous), Telephone Interview, July 1, 2015

Natalya Komarova, Telephone Interview, June 5, 2015

Liddel, Emily, Telephone Interview, July 7, 2015

Linder, Shontal, Telephone Interview, June 25, 2015

McKee, Erin, Telephone Interview, June 30, 2015

McMillon, Carolyn, Telephone and email interview, June 8 & 19, 2015

McNabb, JoAnne, Telephone Interview, June 25, 2015

Radcliffe, Madonna, Telephone Interview, July 8, 2015

Shane, Glynnis, Telephone Interview, June 26, 2015

Shabazz, Alia M, Telephone Interview, July 2, 2015

Smith, Rhonda, Telephone Interview, June 16, 2015

Zimmerman, Ruth, Telephone Interview, July 6, 2015

Websites

http://www.aoa.org/patients-and-public/caring-for-your-vision/comprehensive-eye-and-vision-examination/recommended-examination-frequency-for-pediatric-patients-and-adults?sso=y

Book Recommendations

- *Fierce Conversation* - Susan Scott
- *It Worked for Me: In Life and Leadership* – Colin Powell
- *Lean In: Women, Work, and the Will to Lead* – Sheryl Sandberg
- *How to Become CEO: The Rules for Rising to the Top of Any Organization* – Jeffrey Fox
- *Good to Great Collections* – Jim Collins
- *The Success Principles* – Jack Canfield and Janet Switzer
- *Putting Things First* – Stephen Covey, A. Roger Merrill, and Rebecca R. Merrill
- *The Effective Executive* - Peter Drucker
- *The 7 Habits of Highly Effective People* – Stephen R. Covey
- *Nice Girls Don't Get the Corner Office* – Lois P. Frankel
- *The Well-Spoken Woman: Your Guide to Looking*

and Sounding Your Best – Christine K. Jahnke
- *Creating Personal Presence: Look, Talk, Think, and Act Like a Leader* – Dianna Boohner
- Harvard Business Review

ABOUT THE AUTHOR

An ambitious young professional, born and raised in Jamaica, West Indies, Chantal moved to the US at a young age and that experience has made her very adaptable and ambitious. Chantal seeks opportunities in all shapes and forms and is motivated by challenges.

As a federal employee, she has been with her agency for over six years, starting as a GS 7 and working her way up the ladder to management. Chantal is the youngest leader among her current management team in her office and she strives to be the best she can be every day.

Chantal Wynter lives by the motto that everything happens for a reason. With this motto, she remains optimistic and searches for the lessons and connections in life. She believes this book was written for a reason and hopes to inspire and help as many future leaders as possible.

Thank you for reading. ☺

www.ingramcontent.com/pod-product-compliance
Lightning Source LLC
Chambersburg PA
CBHW082336110426
42744CB00037B/1040